THE LITTLE BOOK OF GARDENING TIPS

WILLIAM FORTT

THE LITTLE BOOK OF GARDENING TIPS

WILLIAM FORTT

A.
Absolute Press

First published in Great Britain in 2006 by
Absolute Press
Scarborough House, 29 James Street West
Bath BA1 2BT, England
Phone 44 (0) 1225 316013 **Fax** 44 (0) 1225 445038
E-mail info@absolutepress.co.uk
Web www.absolutepress.co.uk

Reprinted 2007.

A catalogue record of this book is available from the British Library

ISBN 13: 9781904573357

Printed and bound in China by 1010 International

Gardens are not made
By singing: 'Oh how beautiful!'
and sitting in the shade.

Rudyard Kipling

1

When planning a garden, think of the paths first. They are the highways of the garden, for wheeling barrows and getting to and from the shed. Don't make them too narrow or longer than necessary just for the sake of it. In the vegetable plot, straight paths are usually the best.

2

It is vital to

know what your soil is made of

before you start.

Is it clay, chalky, sandy, silty or peaty? Ask the neighbours or use a commercial kit to test the pH. You can then decide what grows best in it, and what kind of treatment it needs.

3

Feed the soil.

This may sound obvious, but vegetables, shrubs and other flowering plants take a lot of fertility out of your garden every year. You have to

put something back on a regular basis.

Well-rotted compost and animal manure will do most good. If you can't get a reliable supply of these, use bags of general organic fertiliser instead.

4

Always remember that

colours affect our sense of perspective.

Blue and purple flowers draw our eyes into the distance, and make spaces stretch out. White and yellow flowers seem to be much nearer, and tend to foreshorten spaces.

5

Digging a new vegetable garden? Make it easier in the long run by having narrow beds no more than 1.25m (3'6") wide. This way you can tend to the beds without ever having to tread on them. The soil never gets compacted, and stays looser and easier to work. Narrow beds can be as long as you like, but 6m (20') is about right.

6

When digging out vegetable beds in fresh ground, **you are bound to come across plenty of stones.** Don't just throw them away. Collect them in buckets and spread them out evenly to form the bottom layer of paths around the beds.

7

Do you need a rose to drape over an arch?

The old shrub rose 'Zephirine Drouhin' has two great advantages for this job – it is thornless and it boasts a ravishing scent. Its carmine colouring is not bad either.

8

If you have plenty of room,

grow globe artichokes in your flower border. The plants, from the thistle family, need little looking after and have handsome silvery leaves which appear early in the year. And, of course, they produce one of the most sublime of all vegetables.

9

Dead leaves are

a rich source of fertility

when rotted down, but don't mix them into the compost heap – they'll slow down the composting process. Instead, pile the leaves in a quiet corner and forget about them. After two years they will have rotted down into a solid humus ready for digging into borders and vegetable beds.

10

Empty plastic bottles make

fine barriers

to protect tender seedlings

against the curse of the slug. Remove the bottom from each bottle, then slice off 10cm (4") rings. Set a ring round each seedling. Slugs find the sharp edges too painful to climb over.

11

Brighten up the edges of your lawn

by sewing patches of wild flowers such as cowslips, field poppies, scabious and harebells. But don't simply scatter the seeds on bare earth, because few will ever appear. Sew them in pots and plant out the seedlings. Remember to avoid slicing them with the mower.

12

Take cuttings of lavender in late summer.

This is one of the easiest plants to propagate. Simply snip 10cm (4") lengths from shoots which have no flowers and put them in sandy compost in a pot. Don't let them dry out, and protect from excessive heat and cold. Next spring you'll have enough to give away to friends.

13

Rambling roses grow at an astonishing rate in spring. Tie up the new shoots before they get too long, otherwise they will be tossed about by the wind and damaged. Worse still, they **may catch the unwary gardener in the eye!**

14

Give your non-fruiting fruit trees a shock.

Some trees fail to bear fruit because they are growing too strongly (often the result of overenthusiastic pruning). Scare them into action by pruning some of the roots. Dig a trench round half of each tree, a spit deep and about 10cm (4") from the trunk. Ruthlessly cut through any roots you find, then re-fill.

15

Once they have finished flowering,

give daffodils a chance to recover. Tie a knot in the leaves rather than just cutting them down. Let the bulbs draw back the goodness from the stems and foliage, and gain strength for next year.

16

Golden Rules for Composting No.1:

chop it all up.

The smaller the pieces of material on your compost heap, the quicker and better it will rot down. First place the stuff on a hard surface and chop it into bits with a good sharp spade. Tougher objects, such as sprout stems, need to be bashed with a hammer. Then pile it all into the compost bin.

17

Golden Rules for Composting No.2:

keep turning it.

After a couple of months, empty the compost bin and mix the contents thoroughly with a fork. Then chop it about again with a spade before putting it back in the bin. This will speed up the process and produce a more consistent result.

18

Golden Rules for Composting No.3:

cover it up.

Once the heap is built, cover it with old sacks and bits of old carpet. This will keep the heat in as the rotting process gets going. Put corrugated iron, fertiliser bags or something else waterproof on the very top to keep out the rain.

19

When planting in plastic pots, use **a more gritty mix of potting compost.** Plastic pots don't 'breathe' like the porous clay ones, so water doesn't evaporate so quickly. This means that the compost can easily become sodden with too much watering. More grit **helps** the **water to** pass down to the **the roots more quickly.**

20

If you live in a windy area,

a hedge will give better protection than a solid fence or wall. Solid barriers create turbulence on their leeward side. Hedges, on the other hand, filter the flow of the wind and have a calming effect.

21

Look carefully

when choosing conifers

from garden centres or nurseries. The best specimens should have healthy branches down to ground level, and boast a good definite colour.

Size isn't everything – large trees often suffer during transplanting, whereas smaller ones settle down much more readily.

22

Wondering where to put a greenhouse?

Light is the most important factor. If possible, erect the greenhouse so that the ridge runs east-west. This means that the long south side will get as much sun as possible. Avoid having overhanging branches, which may drop – with disastrous results.

23

Most fruit trees will have been grafted onto rootstocks from tougher varieties. You can spot the joint as a **bulge near the bottom of the trunk.** When you plant the tree, make sure that this joint is at least 10 cm (4") above soil level. Any lower, and the top part may start growing roots.

24

Put out food for wild birds in winter.

The more birds you attract to your garden, the better.

If squirrels nip up the pole to pinch the food from an ordinary bird table, make a hanging one instead. Drill holes in each corner of a plywood rectangle, thread string or wire through, and suspend from a handy branch.

25

Buying seeds can be very expensive:

save seeds

from your vegetables and annuals and

save money.

In early autumn, collect the seeds in paper (not plastic) bags and spread them out to dry in a coolish spot. The slightest moisture will encourage the growth of fungal disease which will ruin the seeds.

26

Give your seeds a longer life

by storing them properly. The trick is to keep them completely dry and cool. Put half-used packets in a screw-top glass jar with a sachet or open container of silica gel to soak up excess moisture. This way, they should keep for three years.

27

Keep your strawberry plants young and fit. At the end of the fruiting season (about July), each plant will have sent out a collection of new shoots, or 'runners'. Pinch most of these out, leaving only the two strongest to grow on for next year.

28

Once they start producing flowers, you must

pick sweet peas regularly.

Fill the house with them, give them to family or friends – if you leave them too long, they will go to seed and stop flowering altogether.

29

Save your ice lolly sticks during the hot summer months.

Collect them and clean them. Next spring they will make perfectly-sized marker pegs. When you sow seeds in a tray or pot, write the plant's name on a stick and shove it in.

30

As winter approaches, you'll probably be lighting a bonfire of stuff which won't break down as compost.

Always check through the bonfire heap carefully before you strike a match. The cosy combination of old leaves and stalks makes perfect sleeping quarters for hedgehogs. So take care with that fork.

31

Virginia creeper is a wonderfully effective and speedy wall-covering.

But it **can spread much faster than you think.**

In autumn, treat it roughly – it will soon recover. Clip away shoots which are invading doors and windows. And remember to clear growths which threaten to block gutters and drains.

32

When you are planting shallots, the tops are often near the surface. These are **an irresistible temptation for birds,** who will twitch them up. So cover the shallot bed with wire netting for two or three weeks, until the roots have taken hold.

33

Leave a patch of lawn **uncut for a few weeks.** You'll be surprised by the colourful plants which appear when they are spared from the mower. Campions, cowslips and cuckoo flowers may emerge along with the usual dandelions and plantains. Baby trees (oaks, ashes, maples) which pop up can be lovingly transplanted.

34

Leave room for variety in your vegetable garden.

Only plant as as much as you need

of each kind of vegetable, thus saving space for something else. For instance, two courgette plants produce quite enough for most households. A whole row of runner beans will swamp you in produce, whereas a smaller 'wigwam' will be easily sufficient.

35

Keep fruit trees happy

by clearing grass and weeds from underneath, which will steal nutrients and moisture. The trunks should be surrounded by a radius of at least 1m (3') of bare earth or (preferably) a nice rich mulch. Be careful not to damage the roots with your fork or hoe.

36

Water plants thoroughly.

Make sure the soil around them gets a good soaking so that the water can work its way right down to the roots. A light sprinkling with the hose every day is worse than useless. In fact it will probably do a double dose of harm – encouraging roots to come to the surface and helping weed seeds germinate.

37

Take time checking over potted plants

in garden centres. Make sure that the foliage looks fresh and healthy. Feel the soil for dampness (this means it's been watered regularly). Don't buy anything that is dried out and wilted, or has overgrown roots straggling out of the bottom of the pot.

38

When trimming a hedge, shape it so that it narrows towards the top. This has two merits. It allows light to the hedge bottom, which encourages thicker growth. And it prevents the hedge from becoming top heavy.

39

Nature rarely draws a straight line.

Sweeping curves will best enhance your garden. Disguise straight fences and walls with climbers, and different sized trees and shrubs. Soften the hard edges of steps and paths with low-growing plants.

40

It's very easy to

repair damaged edges of your lawn. Simply use a spade to cut out a square of turf containing the broken edge. Lift the turf up, turn it round and lay it down again – it should fit perfectly. Finally fill in the damaged part with soil and sow some grass seed.

41

House plants may be part of the furniture, but they still **need regular attention.** Wipe their leaves on both sides with cotton wool to get rid of dust which will clog the pores. Cut back trailing shoots or tendrils before they become scruffy or damaged. If they seem to have stopped growing, give them bigger pots.

42

If you're going away

on holiday, take measures to

keep your house plants moist

and happy. Move plants out of direct sunlight. Pinch out surplus flowers and buds. Put especially vulnerable plants in a sink or plastic bowl and pack soggy newspaper or cloth around them. Best of all, get a neighbour to pop in and water them.

43

Invest in a water butt.

You can collect rainwater for your plants from the roofs of the house, the lean-to, the garden shed or the greenhouse. Water is often in short supply in many areas, and soon many may well be on a water meter – and paying much more. Rain is free.

44

Make your own mini potato patch.

Most back yards have room for a 30cm (12") potato pot somewhere. Put crocks on the bottom, then about 5cm (2") of compost. Stick a potato on top (eyes up) and cover with more compost. As shoots appear, add compost until you reach the rim. After 3 months, empty the pot and harvest the spuds.

45

Sow vegetable seeds thinly to avoid waste.

This isn't as easy as it sounds, because many types of seed are so tiny and light. Try mixing them thoroughly with dry sand first. Then you can simply trickle the mixture out of your hand into the drills.

46

Digging a hole for a tree?

Keep things separate – turf in one place, topsoil in another, and subsoil in another. When the hole is dug, chop up the turf and put it at the bottom, grass side down. After settling the tree in place, fill up the hole with a mixture of compost, topsoil and as much subsoil as you need. Tread down firmly.

47

Spread your snowdrops.

When they have finished flowering and are still ‘in the green’ (with leaves),

dig them up and split the clumps.

Then plant the separated bulbs again with a little slow fertiliser such as bonemeal. They will settle much better than dried bulbs.

48

Give a sucker an even break.

You can

multiply shrubs

such as forsythia, weigela and philadelphus by using the suckers they produce. In autumn, scrape away the soil from the sucker. If it has formed roots, snip it off close to the parent stem and transplant.

49

Here are some

simple rules for pruning fruit trees

for those who find the full instructions rather intimidating. Prune in late autumn or winter (though not stone fruits). Cut out any diseased or dead branches, plus any which cross over their neighbours. Try and keep the centre of the tree as open as possible, to let in light.

50

Plant garlic in early winter.

Divide the bulbs and plant in rows in late October or early November. They need a long slow start to their growth, and benefit from a touch of frost (as long as it doesn't hit the shoots). **Harvest them after the leaves have wilted in July.**

William Fortt

William Fortt is a gardener of long standing, whose cottage garden in Wiltshire, is famed for the beauty of its rare plants and the wonders of its many varieties of culinary and medicinal herbs. He has been an author for more than 30 years, with many books to his name.

THE LITTLE BOOK OF
BARBECUE
TIPS
ANDREW LANGLEY

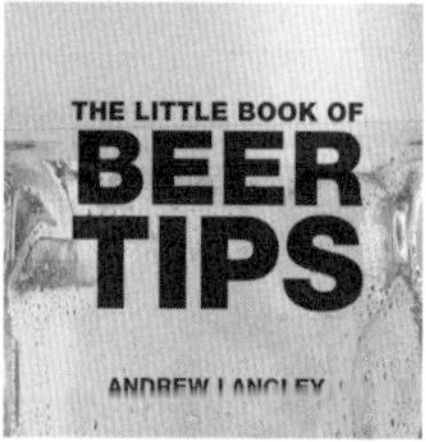
THE LITTLE BOOK OF
BEER
TIPS
ANDREW LANGLEY

THE LITTLE BOOK OF
HERB
TIPS
WILLIAM FORTT

THE LITTLE BOOK OF
POKER
TIPS
PETER FRENCH

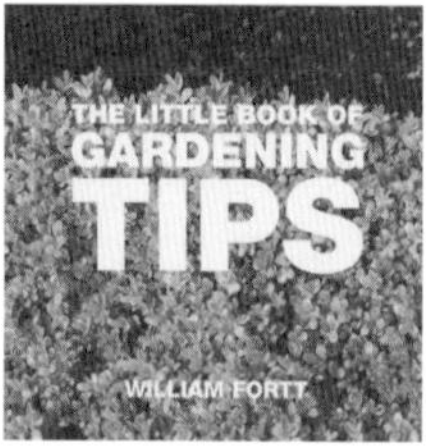
THE LITTLE BOOK OF
GARDENING
TIPS
WILLIAM FORTT

THE LITTLE BOOK OF
CHEFS'
TIPS
RICHARD MAGGS

THE LITTLE BOOK OF
SPICE
TIPS
ANDREW LANGLEY

THE LITTLE BOOK OF
GOLF
TIPS
PETER FRENCH

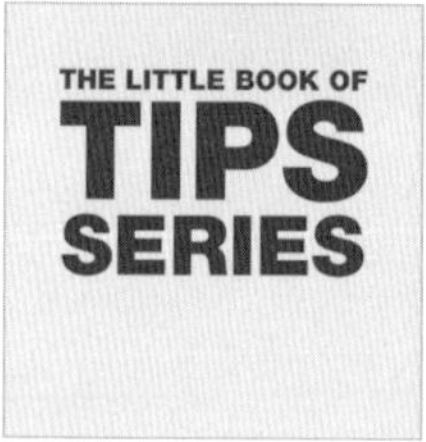
THE LITTLE BOOK OF
TIPS
SERIES

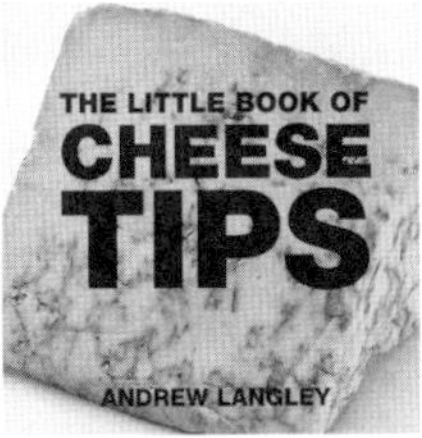
THE LITTLE BOOK OF
CHEESE
TIPS
ANDREW LANGLEY

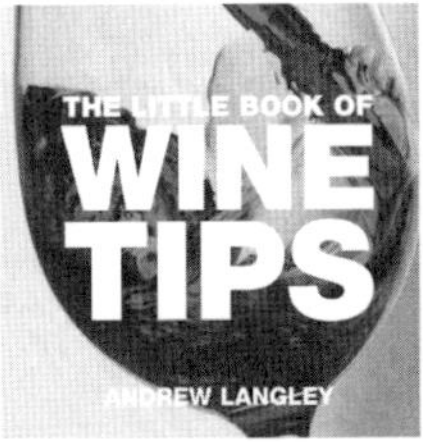
THE LITTLE BOOK OF
WINE
TIPS
ANDREW LANGLEY

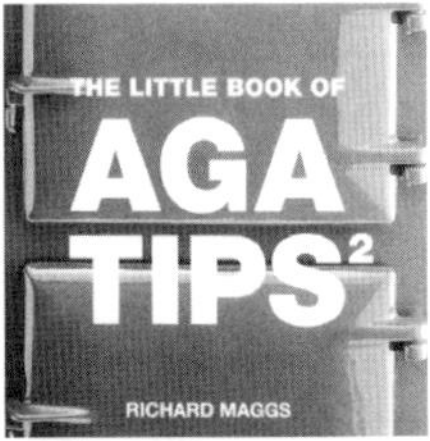
THE LITTLE BOOK OF
AGA
TIPS 2
RICHARD MAGGS

THE LITTLE BOOK OF
COFFEE
TIPS
ANDREW LANGLEY

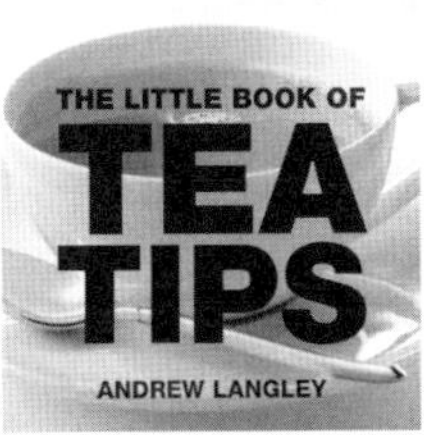
THE LITTLE BOOK OF
TEA
TIPS
ANDREW LANGLEY

THE LITTLE BOOK OF
AGA
TIPS 3
RICHARD MAGGS

THE LITTLE BOOK OF
AGA
TIPS
RICHARD MAGGS

THE LITTLE BOOK OF
CHRISTMAS
AGA
TIPS
RICHARD MAGGS

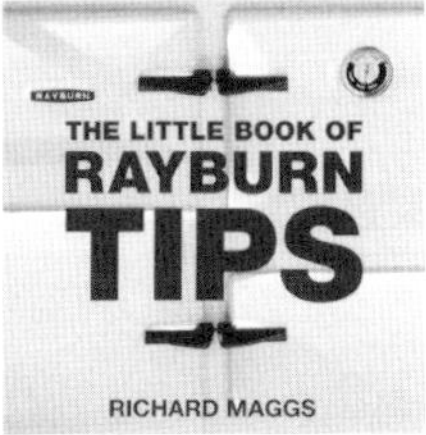
THE LITTLE BOOK OF
RAYBURN
TIPS
RICHARD MAGGS

THE LITTLE BOOK OF
BRIDGE
TIPS

THE LITTLE BOOK OF
CHESS
TIPS
PETER FRENCH

THE LITTLE BOOK OF
FISHING
TIPS

THE LITTLE BOOK OF
GREEN
TIPS
WILLIAM FORTT

THE LITTLE BOOK OF
KITTEN
TIPS
ANDREW LANGLEY

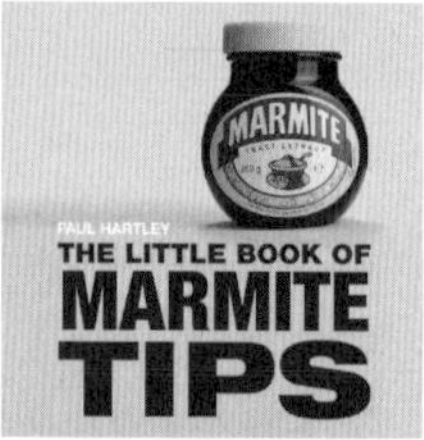
MARMITE
PAUL HARTLEY
THE LITTLE BOOK OF
MARMITE
TIPS

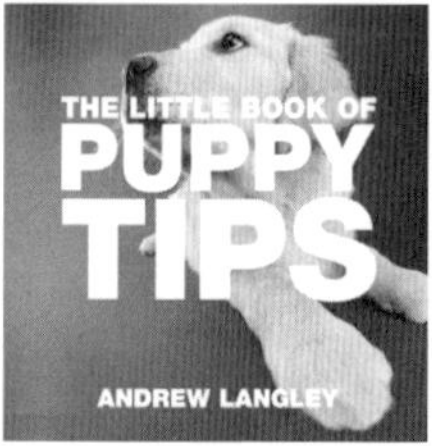
THE LITTLE BOOK OF
PUPPY
TIPS
ANDREW LANGLEY

THE LITTLE BOOK OF
WHISKY
TIPS
ANDREW LANGLEY

THE LITTLE BOOK OF
TRAVEL
TIPS
MEGAN DEVENISH

Little Books of Tips from Absolute Press

Tea Tips
Wine Tips
Cheese Tips
Coffee Tips
Herb Tips
Gardening Tips
Barbecue Tips
Chefs' Tips
Spice Tips
Beer Tips
Poker Tips

Golf Tips
Aga Tips
Aga Tips 2
Aga Tips 3
Christmas Aga Tips
Rayburn Tips
Puppy Tips
Kitten Tips
Travel Tips
Fishing Tips
Marmite Tips
Whisky Tips
Green Tips

All titles: £2.99 / 112 pages

Forthcoming Titles:

Bridge Tips
Chess Tips